THE
REAL
ITALY

Your need-to-know guide
for **all** things Italian

Paolo Messi

FRANKLIN WATTS

First published in 2013
by Franklin Watts

Copyright © Franklin Watts 2013

Franklin Watts
338 Euston Road
London NW1 3BH

Franklin Watts Australia
Level 17/207 Kent Street
Sydney, NSW 2000

Series editor: Sarah Peutrill
Series designer: Sophie Wilkins
Picture researcher: Diana Morris

Dewey number: 914.5

HB ISBN: 978 1 4451 1969 4
Library ebook ISBN: 978 1 4451 2596 1

Printed in China

Franklin Watts is a division of Hachette Children's
Books, an Hachette UK company.
www.hachette.co.uk

Picture credits: Ableimages/Getty Images: 30b.
AFP/Getty Images: 26tr, 27t, 26tl, 28t.
Alessandro770/Shutterstock: 35b. Alexey Arkhipov:
5tl, 7tr, 13tr. The Art Archive/Alamy: 13tl, 42tl.
Lina Balciunaite/Shutterstock : 9tr. O.Bellini/
Shutterstock.: 12c. Bocman1973/Shutterstock:
24-25. Boerescu/Shutterstock: 38b. Anna
Bryukhanova/iStockphoto: 10b. Michele Caminati/
Shutterstock: 38tr, 41t. Diego Cervo/Shutterstock:
front cover bl. P Crucuatti/Shutterstock: 16t, 16c.
Davide D/Shutterstock: 40b. Ian Dagnall/Alamy: 15.
Stefania D'Alessandro/Redferns/Getty Images: 19b.
Erica Donolato/wikipedia: 19t. Edelia/Shutterstock:
1, 11b. Eder/Shutterstock: 2, 8tl. Ermess/
Shutterstock: 6tl, 16tr, 23b. Greg Balfour Evans/
Alamy: 32t. Faberfoto/Shutterstock: 10t. David
Ferreri/Alamy: 17. FooTToo/Shutterstock: 6c,
37t, 48. Sankha Guha/Alamy: 11t. Scott Hortop
Travel / Alamy: 33. Al Kan/Shutterstock: 38tc, 40t.
Mirco Lazzari gp/Getty Images: 28b. Liz Leydon/
istockphoto: 5tr, 12tl, 14t, 42tc. Dave Long Media/
iStockphoto: 10c. LOOK/Robert Harding PL: 12tr,
14b. Lucarelli/Wikipedia: 31t. Georgio Magini/
istockphoto: front cover br. Maisicon/Shutterstock:
30tl,36. Marka/Alamy: 20b. Maudanros/
Shutterstock: front cover bc. Mlenny Photography/
istockphoto: 5tc, 6b, 21. Trevor Neal/Alamy: 22.
Massimo Petranzi/Dreamstime: 5b,30tc,35t, 47.
Yulia Popkova/istockphoto: front cover t. Lorenzo
Puricelli//iStockphoto: 12tc, 12b. M.Rohana/
Shutterstock: 34b. Mr Segui/Shutterstock: 26tc,
29t. Shardan/Wikipedia: 31b. Spirit of America/
Shutterstock: 6tr. Stock Italia/Alamy : 32b.
Superstock/Alamy: 38tl, 39t. Flavio Vallenari/
istockphoto: 6tc. Venturelli/Getty Images: 18.
Vesilivio/Shutterstock: 30tr,34t, 42tr. Claudio Villa/
Getty Images: 26c. vvoe/Shutterstock: 5c, 16tc, 20t.
Wjarek/Shutterstock: 42b.

Every attempt has been made to clear copyright.
Should there be any inadvertent omission please
apply to the publisher for rectification.

CONTENTS

Milan, p.20

Venice, p.35

WHAT'S HOT: ITALY

Beautiful beach in Amalfi, p.37

Italy is a lively country with lots going on. Whether you fancy partying at a music festival, hiking in the mountains, watching the Italian Grand Prix with the world's most fanatical fans, or just hanging out on a beach and eating great food, you'll find it in Italy.

1. VISIT THE HOME OF PIZZA p.12

Naples, a city in the south of Italy, claims to be the home of pizza. Whether this is true or not, the nearby sights make it well worth a visit.

2. PARTY IN SAN REMO p.18

Join the crowds at the week-long San Remo music festival, which happens on the beautiful Italian Riviera in February and March.

3. WINDOW SHOP IN MILAN'S 'GOLDEN RECTANGLE' p.21

Italy is famous for its fashion, and nowhere more so than the northern city of Milan. The 'Golden Rectangle' of designer shops must be one of the most exclusive (and expensive) shopping areas in the world.

4. WALK THE MOVIES-AND-GORE TOUR OF ROME p.24

Spend a day wandering around the blood-soaked historical sites of Rome, with a few movie locations thrown in for light relief.

High fashion in Milan, p.21

5. SPEND A DAY WITH JUVE p.26

Juve (short for Juventus) is Italy's most successful football club. Taking a tram out to the stadium on match day is a great thrill for any football fan.

6. TAKE PART IN YOUR FIRST PASSEGGIATA p.32

Every evening, Italians spill out onto the streets to wander slowly up and down, chat to their friends, and perhaps have a drink or an ice cream. But where's the best place to join in and 'do some laps' with them?

7. VISIT A DECADE VOLCANO pp.13 and 39

Italy is home to not one but TWO of the world's 16 most dangerous volcanoes. Mt Vesuvius is near Naples, and Mt Etna is on the island of Sicily.

Mt Vesuvius, p.13

IT'S (NEARLY) OFFICIAL!
TOP PLACES TO VISIT IN ITALY

Members of one of the world's biggest travel websites picked these top Italian destinations:

1. Rome – the capital city's ancient Roman sites, such as the Colosseum, came out tops.

2. Florence – one of Italy's most beautiful cities, though it can be a struggle to avoid the crowds.

3. Venice – because you can't tour Italy without visiting Venice for a ride in a gondola.

4. Sorrento – known as the 'Land of Mermaids', it's a great place for diving – but also hiking, fishing or just enjoying the view from the cliffs.

5. Taormina – this Sicilian town perches high above the sea. Wander through the twisting streets to the 2,000-year-old Greek theatre.

6. Positano – right in the middle of the Amalfi coast, so you might have to dodge film crews shooting car adverts on the dramatic coastal highway.

ITALY
FACTS AND STATS

The jagged Dolomite Mountains in the Alps, northern Italy

From peaceful river valleys to jagged mountains and buzzing cities, Italy has something for any visitor. And just to add a bit of excitement, it all happens in the shadow of two of the world's most dangerous volcanoes...

LANDSCAPE

Italy has a line of mountains, the Apennines, running all the way down its length. The largest flat area is the Po Valley, in the north. Landscape hotspots to look out for include:

- Deadly volcanoes Mt Vesuvius and Mt Etna

- Italian lakes (great for celebrity spotting – George Clooney has a villa here!)

- Giant sand dunes in the south of the island of Sardinia

- Raganello Canyon, a deep, water-carved canyon in the Calabria region in the south

Key
- ■ Capital city
- ○ Other cities
- ▲ Volcanoes

Map of Italy

CLIMATE

In winter, the high mountains get snow, and the north can be wet and rainy. Further south the weather is almost always warm. Sicily, just about as far south as you can go and still be in Italy, is rarely chilly.

In summer, northern Italy has a perfect climate for hanging out on the beach or eating ice cream in the shade. In the south, though, the heat can be so fierce in July and August that it keeps people indoors. Wildfires are a danger throughout Italy in the summertime.

Fields and mountains in Sicily

"It's the thing I've done ... that has brought me the most joy. It changed everything in my life."

— George Clooney, on buying a villa in Italy

FACT FILE ONE

CAPITAL CITY: Rome

AREA: 294,140 km² of land area, plus 7,200 km² of sea area

HIGHEST MOUNTAIN: Monte Bianco (4748 m), a sub-peak of Mont Blanc

LOWEST POINT: Mediterranean Sea (0 m)

LONGEST RIVER: Po (652 km)

BORDERS: Italy has borders with other countries to the north: France, Switzerland, Austria and Slovenia. Vatican City and San Marino are independent states within Italy.

NATURAL HAZARDS: avalanches, landslides, mud flows, earthquakes, volcanic eruptions, floods

PEOPLE

Italians are very proud of their country, but also of the region they come from. This is probably because until 1861, Italy wasn't a united country. Instead it was made up of lots of different territories, each with its own culture.

Piazza di Spagna, Rome

Almost everyone in Italy speaks Italian, but there are German, French and Slovene-speaking areas in the north.

The biggest division in Italy today is between the north and south of the country. The north is home to most of Italy's businesses, and its people generally have more money. Southern Italy is more agricultural and poorer.

URBAN LIFE

Two out of three Italians live in urban areas, mostly in big cities. Italians are very sociable and like having other people around. That's a good thing, because in the cities most people live in small apartments. Meeting friends and socialising is done outside, in the warm air. The pavements and squares are always full of people meeting friends for a drink, a *gelato* (ice cream) or a slice of pizza.

Pedestrianised street, Naples

Apartment living in Belagio, Lombardy, northern Italy

Caffetteria

An evening market in the countryside

RURAL LIFE

Life is quieter in countryside areas. People who work on the land are up early, rest in the heat of the day and work again in the cooler afternoon and evening. You can never stop Italians socialising, though, so people still meet up to talk and eat together.

Steep streets in Rome

FACT FILE TWO

POPULATION: 61 million

POPULATION: Rome (3.35 million), Milan (2.96 million), Naples (2.27 million), Turin (1.66 million)

AGE STRUCTURE: 13.8% under 15 years old; 65.7% 15–64 years old; 20.5% over 64 years old

YOUTH UNEMPLOYMENT (15–24-year-olds): 25.4%

OBESITY: 9.8%

LANGUAGES: Italian (official language), German, French and Slovene

RELIGIONS: Italy is 80% Christian (almost all Roman Catholic), there are small numbers of Jews and Muslims, and the rest of the population claims no religion

A SLICE OF ITALY

The thing everyone knows about Italy is that it's where pizza comes from. And there's one place in particular that all pizza-loving tourists should visit – Naples. The city takes great pride in being the place that invented pizza.

A SHORT HISTORY OF PIZZA

So how did Naples become famous as the home of pizza (especially as pizza actually came from various places in Italy, not only Naples)?

1. You need a tasty product

The original Neapolitan pizza was just tomato on bread. Later, cheese was added and the bread base changed.

2. Launch an international sales campaign

During the 19th and 20th centuries, many people left Naples to live in other countries, particularly the USA. When they arrived, some opened pizza restaurants.

3. Watch as pizza spreads around the world

Of course, just tomato and cheese wasn't enough. Pretty soon all kinds of toppings were being added. Pizza's global domination had begun.

4. Wait for pizza to come back, like a boomerang

In Naples today, the original bread, tomato and cheese pizza is still around. Just about every other topping can also be found, though.

Pizza preparation

PIZZA IN INDIA

The latest place to become mad about pizza is India. Like everyone else, Indians have adapted the dish to suit their own tastes. You're as likely to get a paneer (Indian cheese) pizza as a margherita!

Underground vaults, Naples

Pompeii with Mt Vesuvius behind

THINGS TO DO IN NAPLES

Of course, eating pizza isn't the only thing you can do while you're in Naples. Here are a few more ideas:

1. Underground Naples – Beneath the city streets is an underground world of hidden passages, caverns and catacombs (above left) filled with the skulls of the dead. Better take a guide...

2. Walk the horses – In Piazza del Plebiscito are two bronze horses. Close your eyes and try to walk between them. Be warned – the slope of the ground makes it tricky!

3. Visit Mt Vesuvius – In CE 79, this volcano destroyed much of the surrounding area including the cities of Herculaneum and Pompeii (above right). Today you can walk on the slopes, but be warned – experts are expecting another eruption soon...

MORNING MARKETS

Mouthwatering market produce in Venice

Every town and city in Italy has a morning food market. These are usually somewhere in the town centre. Wandering around the morning markets, looking at the amazing fresh produce, is one of the best things about Italy.

THE FIRST ESPRESSO

At any market, cafés will be selling caffè (coffee). Usually it's espresso, a small cup of strong coffee. Achille Gaggia invented today's gurgling espresso machines in Italy, in 1937. Italians often drink capuccino in the morning which is espresso, hot milk and steamed-milk foam.

Milky coffee, fuel for the morning.

A DAY'S FOOD

So, what should you buy at the market for a typical day of Italian eating?

For breakfast

Breakfast is usually a hot drink (most often milky coffee), and bread or rolls with butter and jam.

Ready for lunch

A traditional Italian lunch is at least four courses long and takes hours. First come cold meats, little sandwiches, olives and cheeses. Next is a small bowl of pasta, risotto or soup. The third course is meat or fish with a few vegetables or salad. Finally, along comes a sweet dessert or some fresh fruit. Phew!

A little light snack?

These days, not everyone can get two hours off at lunchtime for a giant traditional meal. Mid-afternoon, they start to feel peckish – it's time for 'merenda', an afternoon snack! This is mainly for kids after school, but adults sometimes join in, too.

And finally... dinner

Dinner, which is usually between 19:30 and 21:00, is basically lunch, Part II. People eat lighter food and smaller portions, but it's still four courses long.

> "As they say in Italy, Italians were eating with a knife and fork when the French were still eating each other."
>
> — US chef Mario Batali

FOOD

Lunch in the shade in Como, northern Italy

WAREHOUSE MARKETS

To buy just about anything you can't get at a food market, you can visit a warehouse market. People bring along unwanted possessions for sale, and you can buy anything from kitchens to clothes.

MUSIC

If you travelled round Italy listening only to folk music, you might quickly become confused about which country you're in. Every region seems to have its own style! Fortunately, no one will force you to listen to folk. There's lots of modern music to hear in Italy!

DJ set in an Italian nightclub

TYPES OF MUSIC

Pop isn't the only kind of modern music you'll hear in Italy:

Electronic music is popular: in the 1980s and 90s, the Italian style (called Italo disco) influenced global bands like New Order and the Pet Shop Boys.

Italy has a big hip-hop scene.

Listen out for 'Mediterranean fusion', too. This combines European, Middle Eastern and North African styles.

TRADITIONAL MUSIC –
NORTH AND SOUTH

Traditional music is often played at fairs, weddings and other big celebrations. What you'll hear depends on where you are. In the northeast, waltzes and polkas (which might sound more at home in Eastern Europe) might take you by surprise. Far to the south, the music will make you think of North Africa.

AMICI DI MARIA DE FILIPPI

Wherever you go in Italy, you'll hear young people talking about *Amici* (which means 'friends'). It's a TV talent contest for singers and dancers. In the early stages contestants live in a training camp and their lessons are shown on afternoon TV. Then those who get through to the next stage appear on a weekly evening TV show, competing in teams.

Amici has produced some of the biggest stars in Italian music. In particular, listen out for Emma Marrone and Alessandra Amoroso on the radio, in cafés, on buses – just about anywhere, in fact!

Alessandra Amoroso, winner of *Amici*

CULTURE

"You may have the universe if I may have Italy."

— Guiseppe Verdi, famous Italian composer (1813–1901)

MUSIC FESTIVALS

As you'd expect in a country where people love music, Italy has festivals all through the year. In fact, you could easily spend a whole summer zipping from festival to festival.

● ●

SAN REMO MUSIC FESTIVAL

San Remo takes place at the end of February and in early March. It began after the Second World War (1939–45), as a way of bringing visitors to the seaside resort. Today it's the biggest music festival in Italy.

San Remo is like a combination of Glastonbury Festival and *The X-Factor*: it's a festival, but it's also a competition. The biggest names in Italian music mix with newcomers, and everyone has to perform previously unrecorded songs. The best song, and overall winner, is named at the end.

Emma Marrone celebrates her 2012 win at San Remo

AN, UM... INSPIRATION?

Not many people know this but... San Remo Music Festival was the 'inspiration' (if that's the correct word) for the Eurovision Song Contest. The annual Eurovision Song Contest was first held in 1956, five years after the first San Remo Music Festival.

Italia Wave Love Festival

ITALY FESTIVAL PLANNER

JUNE

Gods of Metal (Milan, northwest Italy)

You really have to like heavy metal to show up at this one. As the name suggests, it's pretty much all you'll hear.

JULY

Italia Wave Love Festival (Livorno, northwest coast)

A six-day festival that's completely free? No wonder it's popular. *Italia Wave* is best known for rock music and upcoming bands, but big stars also play. The music is split between rock, pop, dance and electronica, plus some folk.

JULY

Jammin' (Milan, northwest Italy)

Heavy on the rock and pop, with past headliners including the Red Hot Chili Peppers, but you can also expect a helping of electronica.

SEPTEMBER

I-Day Festival (Bologna, central Italy)

A full-on popfest, held in a field outside the city. It usually boasts a varied line-up of top artists. Past bands have included Arctic Monkeys and Kasabian.

Jammin' festival

FASHION

Most Italians – especially young people – take great pride in their clothes. The winding streets of Italy's ancient city centres are filled with small shops, selling all kinds of fashion gear. There are also plenty of modern stores with famous Italian brands such as Benetton and Armani.

Covered walkways shelter shoppers, Milan

MILAN – ITALY'S FASHION CAPITAL

Milan is at the heart of the Italian fashion and modelling industries. (It's also a centre for banking, which is less interesting.) This must be one of the only places in the world where people actually WEAR the wacky creations that appear on catwalks. The only trouble with Milan is that everyone is so obsessed with getting their beauty sleep, that there's not much going on after about 22:00 at night! Before then, though, it's a great place to watch the beautiful people and the latest fashions.

Posing outside Prada

THE WORLD'S OLDEST MALL?

Milan's Galleria *Vittorio Emanuele II* is one of the world's oldest surviving shopping malls. The glass-roofed arcade first opened in 1867. The Prada store inside began trading just before the First World War, in 1913.

THE GOLDEN RECTANGLE

Milan's Quadrilatero d'Oro (Golden Rectangle) is made up of four of the smartest shopping streets anywhere in the world. You can visit just about any designer store you can name – though actually buying anything will probably require a medium-sized Lottery win.

DESIGNER OUTLETS

Milan is crammed with designer outlet stores, selling cheap designer clothes, if you know where to look. Fortunately, finding them isn't that hard: there's an outlet-store guide, called the *Scopri Occasioni*. The biggest bookshops even have this in English.

> "In Italy they take cheap cloth and make it look expensive. I take expensive cloth and make it look cheap."
>
> — British fashion designer Vivienne Westwood

Versace is one of Italy's most famous fashion houses

OTHER FASHION CITIES

Milan isn't the only Italian city fashion fans will find worth a visit:

1. Rome
Home to famous fashion houses such as Bulgari, Fendi and Valentino. Italy's most fashionable labels have stores in Rome along the Via dei Condotti.

2. Florence
Florence is home to Ferragamo and Gucci, among others. The swankiest shopping street is the Via de' Tornabuoni.

SCOOTER CRAZY!

Scooters weren't invented in Italy, but it's the country that made them famous. After the Second World War (1939–45), Italians needed cheap transport and scooters provided it. They remain just as popular today. Everywhere you go in Italy, there are people whizzing about on scooters.

If you want to look cool, it has to be a Vespa

A (LITTLE BIT OF) SCOOTER HISTORY

A company called Piaggio built the first Italian scooters. Piaggio had been making aircraft, but their factory had been bombed to pieces during the Second World War. They decided to make scooters instead. Soon after, another company, Lambretta, also began making scooters. It wouldn't be long before everyone – from teenagers to little old ladies – was buzzing around Italy on a scooter.

SCOOTERS CONQUER THE WORLD

Scooter sales grew quickly: by 1950, 24 times as many scooters were being sold as in 1947. Then a film called *Roman Holiday* was released. In it, a runaway princess and an American journalist whiz around Rome on a scooter. The film was a massive hit – and so was the scooter. Pretty soon, musicians, actors and cool cats everywhere were riding around on scooters. They still are.

15 MILLION AND COUNTING

By the time it was 50 years old, Piaggio's Vespa company had sold 15 million scooters around the world.

SCOOTER REGULATIONS

You can ride a 50cc scooter at 14 years old in Italy and many kids have one. The coolest scooter by miles is a Vespa, though young people also ride other Italian makes such as Piaggio and Aprilia.

Old, restored scooters parked in Imola, Bologna

'Sembra una vespa!'

— This means, 'It looks like a wasp!' They were the first words Enrico Piaggio said on seeing his company's new scooter design. The name stuck, partly because the buzzing noise of the scooter's engine sounded like a wasp, too.

A COUNTRY OF **RUINS**

As you travel around Italy, you can't help noticing that in amongst all the stylish new concrete-and-glass buildings there are a lot of really very old ones. It's because Italy was home to the Roman Empire, which controlled most of Europe 2,000 years ago.

THE MOVIES-AND-GORE TOUR OF ROME

There are lots of guided tours of Rome, but for something a bit different, give our movies-and-gore tour a try:

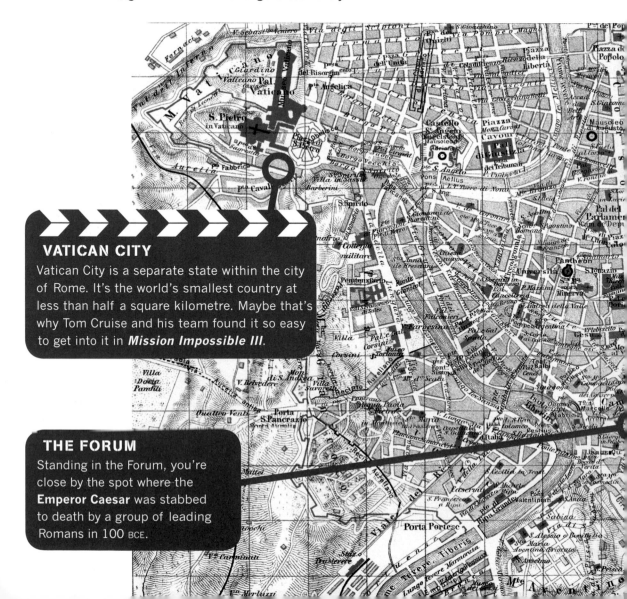

VATICAN CITY

Vatican City is a separate state within the city of Rome. It's the world's smallest country at less than half a square kilometre. Maybe that's why Tom Cruise and his team found it so easy to get into it in *Mission Impossible III*.

THE FORUM

Standing in the Forum, you're close by the spot where the **Emperor Caesar** was stabbed to death by a group of leading Romans in 100 BCE.

HOW ANCIENT ROME WAS
(A LITTLE BIT) LIKE TODAY

Ancient Rome wasn't all togas, gladiators and stuffed dormice (a favourite Roman recipe). They actually had quite a lot of things we'd find familiar...

Apartment blocks – these were often six or more floors high. They fell or burned down worryingly frequently (especially if you lived in one!)

Takeaways – most people lived in tiny rooms with no cooking place, so takeaway food was very popular.

Horoscopes – Romans were very superstitious, and rarely made any big decision without checking their horoscope.

Showers – the shower was invented by Sergius Orata in about 100 BCE and was very popular.

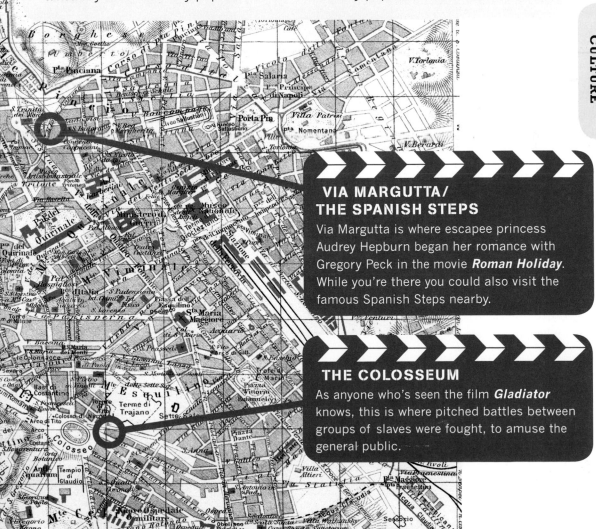

VIA MARGUTTA/ THE SPANISH STEPS

Via Margutta is where escapee princess Audrey Hepburn began her romance with Gregory Peck in the movie *Roman Holiday*. While you're there you could also visit the famous Spanish Steps nearby.

THE COLOSSEUM

As anyone who's seen the film *Gladiator* knows, this is where pitched battles between groups of slaves were fought, to amuse the general public.

GOOAAAAALLLLLL!

Fans gather at Inter Milan

Every big Italian city has a football team. Some, for example Rome, Milan and Turin, have two. If there's a match on when you're visiting, the streets will fill with fans of all ages, heading for the stadium.

MATCH DAY IN TURIN

Turin has two big football teams: Juventus and Torino. Juventus is one of the world's most successful football clubs and it's a great day out to join the crowds going to the match.

1. Catch a tram to the stadium

On match days, there are special trams to Juventus Stadium. If you're going on a non-match day, you have to catch a bus, which is much less fun.

2. Get yourself a Juventus scarf/shirt/hat

Inside the stadium is a small shopping area where you can buy Juventus kit in the famous black-and-white colours.

3. Enjoy the match

Italian fans really get into the game, so there will be singing and chanting all through. If Juve win, the tram ride back to the city will be VERY noisy.

> "I couldn't settle in Italy – it was like living in a foreign country."
>
> – Welsh footballer Ian Rush on his time playing for Juventus

THE JUVENTUS MUSEUM

For hardcore football fans, Juventus Stadium has a museum, telling all about the club's history. You can also take a guided tour of the stadium.

Fanatical Juventus fans

TOP ITALIAN FOOTBALLERS

You could easily fill a whole book with details of great Italian footballers, but today's best include:

Mario Balotelli, AC Milan

Balotelli is almost as famous for his off-field activities (e.g. driving into a women's prison 'to have a look around') as his skills as a striker.

Gianluigi Buffon, Juventus

One of the world's top goalkeepers, Buffon captains both Juventus and the Italian national team.

Daniele de Rossi, Roma

Born in Rome, and playing for the city's big club, de Rossi was Italian Footballer of the Year in 2009. He's one of the world's best midfielders.

Antonio di Natale, Udinese

In the 2010–11 season, di Natale's strike rate was 0.78 goals per game, third best in Europe, behind Christiano Ronaldo and Lionel Messi.

MOTOR RACING

If there's one thing Italians – especially Italian men – love almost as much as football, it's motor racing. The fanatical Italian motor racing fans are known around the world as *tifosi* (which is actually just Italian for 'fans').

First lap of the Italian Grand Prix

Motor-racing fans at the Italian Grand Prix

CAR RACING

In September, the world's biggest car-racing league arrives at the Autodromo di Monza, near Milan. For three days the whole area is crammed with people wearing red Ferrari T-shirts, jackets and hats. They're here for the Formula 1 Italian Grand Prix. They will all be hoping that Ferrari, Italy's most famous racing team, can pull off a home win.

VALENTINO ROSSI

Italy's Valentino Rossi is probably the greatest motorbike racer ever. By 2012 he had been world champion nine times, and won 105 top-class races.

Rossi is so famous in Italy that for a while he was forced to move to London, to get away from the crowds of fans!

MOTORBIKE RACING

In Italy, motorbike racing always draws a crowd. The year's big races begin with the World Superbike race at the Monza racetrack, in May. World Superbike returns in June, for a race at the Imola circuit. Also in June, MotoGP, the world's top bike-racing league, arrives for a race at Mugello. MotoGP returns in September for the San Marino race.

Of course, it's not only big races that attract crowds. All through the year there are smaller races at Italy's famous tracks. For bike-racing fans, it's always worth joining the tifosi at the Imola, Misano, Monza and Mugello racetracks.

Q: WHEN IS A RACE IN SAN MARINO NOT IN SAN MARINO?

A: Nearly always. The San Marino Grand Prix is held at Imola (in the Bologna region) and the San Marino MotoGP and Superbike races happen at the Misano circuit (near Rimini)!

FAMILY FIRST

Italian families are usually very close, and spend a lot of time together*. Family ties are more important than any others. If you're lucky enough to be welcomed into an Italian family, all the attention can be a bit overwhelming at first!

*One exception might be Giancarlo Casagrande and his daughter, Marina. In 2010, a court ordered Giancarlo to carry on paying Marina her allowance of €350 a month – even though she was 32 years old!

• •

SUNDAY LUNCH

Traditionally, Italian children live close to their parents even after they have left home. On Sundays, the whole family tries to get together for lunch – in fact, over 90% of Italians do this. Often it's a big party, with the extended family – cousins, nephews, nieces and others – all turning up. Lunch can be a long affair, which takes hours and has seven, eight or even more courses.

Italians tend to go out of their way to buy Italian food wherever possible. Each region has its own cooking traditions and every town and village has its own specialities.

Dishes made with fresh, simple ingredients

FOODS TO TRY...

Here are some Italian delicacies you might not have heard of:

CIECHE FRITTE

Popular in coastal resorts as a starter, this is shallow-fried baby eels

JOTA

A bean-and-bacon stew from the northeastern corner of Italy

PANELLE

Fried chickpea burgers, a very popular street food in Sicily

Panelle

... AND FOODS TO AVOID
(UNLESS YOU'RE BRAVE)

And here are a couple of things unwary visitors to Italy might prefer to avoid:

CASU MARZU

This is a maggoty cheese. If someone offers you some, watch out – it's only considered safe to eat if the maggots are alive!

Maggoty cheese – not for everyone

LAMPREDOTTO

It sounds OK in Italian – "Would you like some lampredotto?" Think hard before you say yes: it's actually a tripe sandwich. That's tripe, the lining of a cow's stomach...

FRIENDS

Next to family, Italians treasure their friends. This is especially true of young people. A lot of their leisure time is spent just hanging out with friends, talking about clothes, admiring each other's scooters, arguing about which team is better, Juventus or Milan, and talking about music.

Meeting up with friends

THE PASSEGGIATA

If an Italian says to you 'Andiamo a fare qualche vasca!', you've been honoured. It means 'Let's go and do some laps', and is an invitation to join them for the passeggiata.

The passeggiata is a daily ritual of meeting up with friends for a walk. It happens in every city, town, village and hamlet – anywhere there are more than two or three houses, there will be an evening passeggiata. People dress up in their best clothes and walk slowly around the main square or street. They chat and greet others and often stop for a gelato (ice cream) or a drink.

The passeggiata

BEST PLACES TO WATCH/ JOIN THE *PASSAGGIETA*

Every town and village in Italy has a passaggieta, but these are some of the top spots to join the action:

Rome:
Piazza Navona

Not the only place in Rome to take an evening wander, but the artists, actors and musicians probably make it the liveliest.

Florence:
Piazza della Repubblica

Wandering through the narrow streets to this grand square is a nice, cool walk in the evening heat.

Siena:
Torre del Mangia

This is a spot for watching, instead of joining in. Climbing the 400 steps to the top of the 'Tower of the Eater' gives you a fabulous view of the passaggieta below.

TOP ICE CREAM

Can anywhere in the world have as many ice-cream shops (called *gelateria*) as Italy? If you fancy eating an ice cream as you stroll, here's some top tips for getting the best possible gelato:

1. Check the colour: e.g. a banana flavour should be banana coloured, not fluorescent yellow

2. Look for signs saying *produzione propria* (made on site) and/or *artigianale* (made the old-fashioned way and with natural ingredients)

3. Avoid plastic tubs: if the ice cream is in a plastic container, it has probably been mass-produced

LEISURE

Picking ice cream is a serious business

FESTIVALS

Crazy costume for the Venice Carnival

I n general, Italians love a party or celebration. Maybe that's why there are so many festivals, of all different kinds. They range from small village fêtes to giant, citywide carnivals that last for weeks. If you're in the area when any of these take place, hold on to your hat – they can be pretty wild!

FEBRUARY:

Carnevale
(Venice and elsewhere)

Many Italians take part in Lent, 40 days when Christians eat and drink less than usual. Carnevale is a festival that happens before Lent. It's a last chance to have a blowout party. The biggest celebrations are in Venice, where people dress in fantastic outfits and wear scary masks. There are also big Carnevale celebrations in Viareggio.

JULY/AUGUST:

Palio (Siena)

If you've seen the Bond movie *Quantum of Solace*, you already know what the Palio looks like: it appears almost at the start of the film. It's a crazy horse race around the fan-shaped central square. The contest is between riders from Siena's 17 ancient neighbourhoods.

The Palio in full swing

JUNE:

Regatta of the Ancient Maritime Republics
(location changes)

Between about 900 and 1300 CE, Italian cities built great fleets for trading and war. These cities were called the Maritime Republics. Each year, a rowing race is held between crews from four of the Republics (Amalfi, Genoa, Pisa and Venice). The race is the centrepiece of a big festival and parade.

The Republics take it in turns to be host: in Amalfi and Genoa the race is in the sea, in Pisa it happens on the River Arno, and in Venice (left) the rowers race in the Venice Lagoon.

OTHER FESTIVALS

Saint's Day

Almost every town and village in Italy has a patron saint. If you time your visit to a place so that you're there on the saint's special day, there will probably be a festival of some sort, with food, drink and music.

Flower fesivals

Many towns hold flower festivals in May or June. Petals are used to create amazing works of art such as this one in Genzano (right).

LEISURE

BEACH LIFE

One of the best things about a visit to Italy is the beaches. In July and August they are lively places, with busy cafés and restaurants open into the night. At other times the beaches are quieter – in winter you might even get a stretch of sand completely to yourself.

ITALY'S BEST BEACHES

There are thousands of beaches in Italy, and it can be tricky to decide which area to visit. This list will get you started:

1. Liguria (northwest)

The Ligurian coast is a continuation of the French Riviera, and is just as swanky. The region of the Cinque Terre, or Five Lands, is beautiful; if you want more of a city vibe, head along the coast to San Remo.

2. Capri (southeast)

Capri was the ultimate cool place to take a holiday in the 1960s. The beautiful beaches and clear water of this small island in the Tyrrhenian Sea are still pulling in the crowds.

3. The Amalfi Coast (south)

The little towns cling to the cliffs and you climb down steep steps to the beaches. The best way to get from place to place is by boat.

4. Maddalena Archipelago, Sardinia

Most Italians say that Sardinia has the country's best beaches. The Maddalena Archipelago is so beautiful that it has been made a national park.

5. Gargano Peninsula (south)

The beaches near the port of Gallipoli have something for everyone. Close to town they're lively and noisy, but further away there are more monasteries and castles than cafés.

Beautiful clear water in Capri

The steep Amalfi coast

BEACH WORDS

Going to the beach is a typical Italian activity – so it's surprising that so many beach words have been borrowed from English:

posare — to pose

fare jogging — jogging

beach volley — beach volleyball

pic-nic — picnic

lo snorkelling — snorkelling

andare in topless — go topless bathing

la spiaggia nudista — nudist beach

'THAT'S MY (ANCESTORS') SUN LOUNGER'

During August, Italy's beaches can become amazingly crowded. Space is hard to find, and people often have to pay for somewhere to lie. The best spots are highly sought-after. In fact, some families have had the same sun-lounger spots in their family for decades!

SICILY

If Italy is shaped like a long boot, Sicily is the football it's kicking. The island is so far south that it's closer to the coast of North Africa than it is to Rome. Sicily is the largest island in the Mediterranean Sea. You could fit Rhode Island, the smallest state in the USA, into Sicily eight times.*

*Sicily, 25,711 km²; Rhode Island, 3,140 km².

· ·

Baroque church in Catania in the east of Sicily

A MEDITERRANEAN CROSSROADS

Sicily is at the centre of the Mediterranean, dividing west from east, and north from south. The island has been invaded from all sides, by (in order): ancient Greeks, Romans, German Vandals, Turks, North Africans, Normans, more Germans, the French, Austrians, Spanish and French again. Finally, in 1860, the Italian hero Giuseppe Garibaldi landed with an army of 1,000 men and captured the island. After this it became part of a new country – Italy.

Most of the people who invaded and settled in Sicily have left something behind. There are ancient Greek temples and theatres (opposite), Roman mosaics and French baroque buildings. The saffron used in Sicilian cooking first came from Arab traders and the traditional meat dishes arrived with the Norman invaders.

Ancient Greek theatre, Naxos

MT ETNA, DECADE VOLCANO

Decade Volcanoes are the world's 16 most dangerous. They are big volcanoes close to large human settlements. Mt Etna on Sicily is one of two in Italy (the other is Mt Vesuvius, which is 9 km east of Naples). It is one of the world's most active volcanoes: there are lava flows and puffs of volcanic ash almost all the time.

TOP SICILY MOVIES

Sicily has featured in lots of movies. Those that are on TV fairly often include:

Cinema Paradiso – the story of a small boy and a cinema in a remote village.

Big Blue – this film about freediving is set partly in the Sicilian town of Taormina.

Il Postino, filmed partly on Salina, one of the Aeolian Islands, lying just north of Sicily.

AWAY FROM THE MAINLAND

SARDINIA

Popular Sardinian seaside resort of Stintino

Sardinia is the second largest island (after Sicily) in the Mediterranean Sea. In the past, Germans, Italians, the Spanish, Austrians and French have each controlled the island. Finally, in 1861, Sardinia became part of a new country, Italy.

NATURAL ATTRACTIONS

Sardinia has high mountains, deep gorges, steep cliffs and beautiful coves and beaches.

The beaches of Sardinia draw visitors from around the world, and hiking in the mountains is also popular. Visit in August and you'll have a chance to see the Regata della Vela Latina: traditional sailboats from around Italy visit the town of Stintino (above) to race each other.

The Su Gorroppu gorge is especially worth a visit. Walking across a certain piece of land there is said to guarantee you a long life. The trouble is, no one knows exactly where it is...

Su Gorroppu gorge

Rock climbing, Sardinian coast

A DIFFERENT LAND

Sardinia is a very distinctive part of Italy. Its food includes wild boar roasted over a spit, pork-and-bean stews and strong cheeses. Most adult Italians drink wine, but in Sardinia beer is popular. The island's musical life includes an unusual style of multi-toned singing, guitar songs and distinctive dance. People's favourite sports include darts and Sardinian wrestling, which are not common in the rest of Italy.

LANGUAGES

Sardinia's mixed past is clear from the different languages you hear being spoken there:

Italian is heard everywhere;

In different parts of the island Sardinian, Sassarese (a Corsican–Sardinian language) and Gallurese (a variety of Corsican), are all co-official languages;

In the city of Alghero, Catalan (a Spanish language) is spoken alongside Italian;

In the far southwest, a few people still know Friulian, which was brought by settlers from the far northwest of Italy in the 1920s.

OTHER ISLANDS

Italian islands worth visiting include:

The Aeolian Islands, north of Sicily, have active volcanoes on Stromboli and Vocano;

The Phlegraean Islands, in the Bay of Naples, can be visited for a day on a boat from the city;

Elba is the largest island in the Tuscan Archipelago, between the mainland and Corsica.

AWAY FROM THE MAINLAND

KEY INFORMATION
FOR TRAVELLERS

LANGUAGE

English is spoken in many tourist areas, but in general it's best to try to remember a few words of Italian. Even just *salve* (hello), *per favore* (please), *si* (yes), *no* (no), and *grazie* (thank you) will show people you are trying!

ENTERING ITALY

People from European Union countries can enter Italy without a visa, though arrivals at airports and ferry ports usually have to show their passport.

Visitors from other countries may need a visa, so it is important to check with your own government whether this is required.

GETTING AROUND

Italy has a good railway system connecting its cities and towns. The train company is called Trenitalia. Buses are available in large cities and towns, though in rural areas they may not come often, if at all. Cycling is a good way to get around, since regional trains usually take bikes (the departure board should have a bike symbol on it if the train will).

Railway station in Cinque terre, Liguria

HEALTH

Pharmacies, which you can spot by the green cross outside, are a good source of help with minor health problems, though finding a pharmacist who speaks English may be tricky.

If you need to see a doctor in Italy, you have a choice between state or private doctors. In the south, those who can afford it usually go to private doctors or hospitals. In the north, the state service is more popular.

POSTAL SERVICES

The main postal service in Italy is provided by Poste Italiane. You can buy stamps at post offices and tabacchi, small shops with a sign showing a white 'T' on a brown background. The post can be slow: within Italy things take up to a week, and international mail can take twice as long.

Italian post trivia: there's a long list of things you may not send by post in Italy. The list includes spare parts for weapons, articles made of human hair, typewriter ribbons and playing cards.

MOBILE NETWORKS

The main European mobile-phone networks are all available in Italy. Using a foreign phone – even on the same network as you have at home – is expensive, especially for data, so it's important to turn off data roaming.

INTERNET PROVISION

Italy is slowly catching up with Internet provision, but is still behind some other countries. Wifi zones are available in hotels and cafés but you have to get a pass code and log in with your passport number to use them, and it is not always free. Cybercafés offer paid Internet access; public libraries often offer it free or for a small charge.

PUBLIC HOLIDAYS

Most shops and businesses close on these days – Italy is a Catholic country and most public holidays are religious celebrations:

1 January	New Year's Day
6 January	Epiphany
17 March	Unification Day
the Monday after Easter	Easter Monday
25 April, celebrating the liberation of Italy in the Second World War	Liberation Day
1 May	International Workers' Day
1 June, celebrating the birth of the Italian Republic in 1946	Republic Day
15 August	Ferragosto
1 November	All Saints Day
8 December	Feast of the Immaculate Conception
25 December	Christmas Day/Natale
26 December	St Stephen's Day/St Etienne

THE ESSENTIALS

CURRENCY:

Euro (€1 = roughly £0.80, or $1.30). Currency exchange at some banks, *bureau de change*, and train stations.

TIME ZONE:

Central European Time (CET): Greenwich Mean Time (GMT) +1 hour

In March, Italy switches to daylight-saving time, and clocks are put forward one hour. In October they are returned to CET.

TELEPHONE DIALLING CODES:

To call Italy from outside, dial your country's exit code plus 39, and drop the zero.

To call another country from Italy, add 00 and the country code of the place you are dialing to the beginning of the number, and drop the zero.

OPENING HOURS:

Opening hours tend to be different in the city from the countryside (where shops are open less). As a rough guide, most shops open at 09:00 and close again at about 13:00. In the afternoons they will be open between 15:30 and 19:30. Almost all shops close on Sundays outside the major cities.

USEFUL PHRASES:

Buon giorno/Buona sera	Good morning/Good afternoon or evening.
Parla Inglese?	Do you speak English?
Mi scusi	Excuse me.
Prego	You are welcome.
Dove posse trovare un...	Where can I find a...?
Dov'é...?	Where is... ?
Quanto costa?	How much does it cost?

FINDING OUT MORE

BOOKS TO READ: NON-FICTION

EDGE: Mad, Bad and Just Plain Dangerous: Romans John Townsend (Franklin Watts, 2013)
Gruesome and otherwise astounding facts from ancient Rome.

Countries in Our World: Italy
Ann Weil (Franklin Watts, 2012)

This book examines Italy's physical features, daily life, industry, media, leisure and much more.

Destination Detectives: Italy
Paul Mason (Raintree, 2006)
Basic facts about Italy, but presented in the form of a survival guide: how do you get home if you suddenly find yourself stuck in the middle of the country?

BOOKS TO READ: FICTION

Roman Mysteries series by Caroline Lawrence (Orion Children's).
The adventures of a group of kids living in ancient Rome are a great introduction to the empire that once governed most of Europe.

The Thief Lord
Cornelia Funke (2000)
This novel was made into a movie with the same name in 2006. It tells the story of two brothers who run away to Venice, Italy, and fall in with a gang of child thieves.

The Undrowned Child
Michelle Lovric (Orion, 2010)
Another book set in Venice, but a fantasy version of the city where ghosts patrol the streets and librarians turn magically into cats. If you like this, the author has written other excellent novels set in Italy.

WEBSITES

www.italia.it/en/home.html
This is the official Italian Government tourist guide to Italy, and is packed with useful information about places to visit. Clicking the 'Discover' tab and then using the interactive map is a great starting point.

http://tinyurl.com/2zud7w
This link will take you to the CIA (Central Intelligence Agency) web page about Italy. It's quite dry, but crammed full of useful information and statistics.

www.worldtravelguide.net/italy
An excellent site for basic information about travelling in Italy, including practical information about weather, geography, and places to stay, plus ideas for places to visit.

Note to parents and teachers:
Every effort has been made by the Publishers to ensure that these websites are suitable for children, that they are of the highest educational value, and that they contain no inappropriate or offensive material. However, because of the nature of the Internet, it is impossible to guarantee that the contents of these sites will not be altered. We strongly advise that Internet access is supervised by a responsible adult.

THE ESSENTIALS

INDEX